# LET'S GO BACK TO THE MAINLAND

## Grzegorz Wróblewski

### Translated from the Polish by Agnieszka Pokojska

Červená Barva Press
P.O. Box 440357
W. Somerville, MA 02144-3222

www.cervenabarvapress.com

Bookstore: www.thelostbookshelf.com

Cover Photo: Wojciech Wilczyk

Cover Design: William J. Kelle

ISBN: 978-0-9910091-7-6

Library of Congress Control Number: 9780991009176

Distributed by Small Press Distribution: www.spdbooks.org

## ACKNOWLEGMENTS

Some of these poems have previously appeared in:
*Jacket Magazine, Lyric Poetry Review, Poetry Wales, West Wind Review, Eclectica Magazine, The Delinquent, The Journal, Cambridge Literary Review, Postmodern Culture, Words Without Borders, Past Simple, 3:AM Magazine, Otoliths, Exquisite Corpse,* and in the anthology *Carnivorous Boy Carnivorous Bird.*
Our thanks to the various editors

The poems first published in the chapbook *A Rarity* (Červená Barva Press 2009):
*\*\*\* one night, looking, Tide, The Cascade, The Polygon Of Magic, In The Queen's Honor, Jan Hansen's Father, Loyal Friends, Silent Night, Holy Night, The Commandery (At The Brothel At Christine's), \*\*\* The nine holes of my mortal friend, Caution, The Robots Are Come!, Unofficial Code Of Conduct, Suggestion For A June Activity, Mr. Cullen's Raid, A Strange Je Ne Sais Quoi, Toll-gate, A Rarity, Mao, Heartfelt Advice From A Nuuk Fortuneteller, Therapy, The Demons Of Márquez, A Long Friendship, The Breathing Organs Of Fish*

# CONTENTS

# LET'S GO BACK TO THE MAINLAND

## These Special People

I read to him about the Tlingit People
and he
kept throwing sticky
salamanders at me

I spread madness – he added

Also, the way you carry the gooseberry-
filled buckets is all wrong,
as if they were full of water

The world lacks in lightness –

You will fall apart,
You all lack in lightness.

## Summation Schema (On The Illness Of John T.)

The general state of mind?
A pimp and a carpet salesman live in this house.
Neither can stand Dante.
That's because
they never read a line of his.
That's because we're swamped by entertainment literature and life
is utterly devoid of the comic element.
And that has nothing to do with the mannerism of ideas.

A punchline style or classically deformed speech are in.
As for content, all that is secular, prehistoric.
But wait... no!
The pimp did hear of Virgil.
When the old script was stolen.
Very likely he imagined that was Caligula's white steed.
Why am I so bitter?
It would be the same anywhere:

Even
if someone knew Cervantes from cover to cover,
he would never think of
devoting himself to Diderot or, say,
the summation schema in Panfilo Sasso.

**"Controlled Zones," The Zenith Gallery,
Copenhagen (April-May 2009)**

Dear visitor, why do only two of these paintings
remind you of a wild rabbit hunt?

1.
Because I'm old, so old that I didn't have the strength
to ram my paintbrush through the window displaying
biodynamic carrots.

2.
(Forget three-dimensional. The sea merges into clouds
and the foliage unexpectedly changed hue – a megalith,
the abolition of mammals suddenly became fiction…)

3.
Because there's something peculiar about rabbits.
They're just too cute. Danish teenagers keep them as pets, shortly
before getting pregnant.

## Discovering New Lyrical Situations

I sprouted forearms,
one with an outline of a watch.
(The ladies around me
instantly shed their hair.)

\*\*\*

one night, looking
out of the window
you cried: the moon!

frightened as if
you saw it for
the last time ever

## Rooms And Gardens

They will greet you with mysterious
smiles, those who were there before you.
Later, when new ones arrive, you will already
know it all.

You will welcome them with the same smile and
show them in.
With a sweeping gesture you will present
the freshly made beds and the expansive view of the gardens.

At last, when they will have composed themselves a little,
you will explain
where they are and what the future has in store for them.

## Tide

Our birds now circle above other heads.
You're right, the taxes we pay are too high
and the sky has suddenly lost its depth.
The birds were quick to notice...

(Your cold hand touches my parched
skin.) Did I make love to you only
thanks to a full set of teeth and five-digit
extremities?

## The Cascade

The waterfalls are hiding somewhere here – you are feverish
and I open the windows wide every night
believing
that we'll finally hear the roar of water crashing on the rocks.

Meanwhile
there's the insomnia and the silence of the hills. (Our pet lizards
are perilously putting on weight…)
We're slowly taking root in the sands.

## The Polygon Of Magic

That's Nordic forests for you!
says Allan and points at
a slumbering distant rock
which suddenly begins
to rise! I rub
my tired eyes… I am
a believer. I've always lived
around a TV.

**We Will Always Remember The Galleons**
**(Vale Tudo, Acknowledgments: Google & Packard Bell)**

Victoria Beckham
has small tits again:
Craig Rog Call on my mobile +226 783 587 76
Andres Garriz AUSTRALIAN LOTTERY 2009
WINS!!! 1 MILLION POUNDS. CONTACT STEVE BAKER
FOR CLAIMS!
Vale tudo: I was looking straight ahead.
Enter,
smash,
exit.
Sarah Compaq Promo Wins!!! TICKET NUMBER 001768432463
(PHONE: +447035966416)!
ONLINE NOTICE Congrats.
Stakes:
200,
300,
500!
Nielsen vs Nielsen.
Modern karate vs the monastery.
500,
600!
It will be no jiyu kumite.
Nielsen is short of one ear for a start.
He hit someone on the head.
Sarah Compaq Promo Wins!!! TICKET NUMBER 001768432463
(PHONE: +447035966416)!
ONLINE NOTICE Congrats.
Funakoshi would clear off, beaten to a pulp. With his tongue
ripped out. I did just that, clear off. (He would have too.)
Sarah Compaq Promo Wins!!! TICKET NUMBER 001768432463
(PHONE: +447035966416)!
ONLINE NOTICE Congrats.
Morris Totoh NAME: MR. MORRIS TOTOH
Andres Garriz AUSTRALIAN LOTTERY 2009
I bit off a meaty chunk of that Russky today.
Sarah Compaq Promo Wins!!! TICKET NUMBER 001768432463

(PHONE: +447035966416)!
ONLINE NOTICE Congrats.
Morris Totoh NAME: MR. MORRIS TOTOH
Andres Garriz AUSTRALIAN LOTTERY 2009
AUSTRALIAN LOTTERY 2009
"You'll have to fight someone who knows a bit of the White Crane
technique."
"A Chinaman?"
"Your future depends on it."
Craig Rog Call on my mobile +226 783 587 76
The Aabenraa Monster vs the Odense Crane.
"Yeah, but what's the prize?"
That thing looked like a juiced-up man. It had a hole and tits.
(Victoria Beckham
has small tits again)
But other than that, it looked like a man.
Craig Rog Call on my mobile +226 783 587 76
Craig
Rog
Call
on
my
mobile
+226 783 587 76
LOTTERY 2009

A heavily made-up roid-head.
Congrats.

## On The Milky Way

What bliss, to do nothing!
To ignore those who deliver letters or count constellations
for money.

Stroking a stray Alsatian, I look into his
cunning eyes.
He understands me through and through.

He doesn't have to hunt the duck and no one forces him to play
with a rubber bone.
Like me, he relaxes among the unthinking
dandelions.

He seems to think he got what his short mission was about.

## Loyal Friends

Sometimes it's a woman with a fake diamond earring,
at other times a talking parrot or disgraced politician.
My uncle often used to host a priest and a professor
of corpse preservation. They played poker together
and drank *crème de menthe*. That felt good.
I also knew a man who chose solitude.
(He developed a liking for silence and wall-crawling
vermin.) Dying, he left his body as an heirloom.
A massive bloke, he lasted for months and months.

## Together

species
that's me and him

if the two of us together
then count me
out

**Anything Goes (Backing Up A Candidate)**

*Panikon deima...* Acid rains will fall, a dragon
will kidnap us and fly us to Hawaii.

*You can be saved, too.*
The woman handing out the leaflets has the body of a jellyfish,
all see-through,
I can see the Perseids and a boar through it,

a bunch of naked guys (the staff of Piccola Italia?) swarming
around Jytte,
the daughter of the local king Ladon.

The flutes of Amager.
Here comes the long-awaited Lord.

*You can be saved, too,*
All you need to do is register. Sign here
and you will at last

be saved.

## World Record In Deep Diving

The futile wait for Jon K.
(He hadn't been talked into it.)

## Richard's Head

The last in the line of ship welders: Torso Man –
there was an accident and a swelling,
shit luck, as he says.
*You'll learn to walk on your hands in no time,*
they said after he had one leg amputated.

Then,
When they took the other,
It turned out it had been all his fault, too many cheap fags.
It's a mystery why they chopped the arms off too.
All Richard mentions
are the legs. (And we prefer not to pry.)

We push the wheelchair. The earth wiggles its big toe.
Under the bridge we get some reflexive vibes:
*It must have been the Lord's wish!*
(Squirrels pass us by, disgusted…)

He drinks to stupor,
scorns poetry and dried dates.
He still has a bit of a body left and a heavy, flagstone-bruised
head.

## In The Queen's Honor

A friend of mine loathes the hills in the forest.
When he sees one, he always stops and prods it
With a stick. Then he gets a new haircut and quickly
Moves to another apartment. But he can't help
Hearing them come closer. Marching up the stairs.

## Lyrical Poets Haven't Featured In My Poems For A Long Time, So

The lord of cellar labyrinths, the one-eared cat Jespar, fetches
newly hunted young birds to his lair. Men proudly
point him out to their children.
Is he the one that ensures balance in the natural world?, asks Janni.
Yes, he's the one that will save us from poetry, explains her father,
an ardent opponent of social democrats.

## Terrain

The fat lady cashier from Brugsen, four times,
Pierre, the poet and local drunk, five times,
my neighbor Christiansen, surely a hundred times,
a fat Pekinese (that keeps growling at me),
ten times or so,
his owner too, then, ten times or so,
and Mr Paki there at the kiosk, countless times.
Come to think of it… they must have too,
if I have, so many times, then so have they.
How many times, I wonder?

## Cindy's Cradle

Watch out for the traffic, man! – I shouted
and all he replied was,
she was supposed to wear pink tights and
gorge on melons with me

Cindy, Cindy!
You should visit your old man sometime

Look at him now
losing his head on the safety island
surrounded by police and angels
from parallel worlds.

## At Bjarne's Gym

The boys at Bjarne's —
these carefree bruisers

who, panting heavily,
work on their calves today,

all they can think of is
CHROMIUM PICOLINATE.

## A Vermeer Motif

The vision of a deserted city (used a razorblade today?).
We finished screwing a whole army of greenish
cooks from Amager
and then

the Kamasutra moved
into a Chinese fireworks shop. The monstrosity of man!
You can't paint
that.

## Jan Hansen's Father

Jan Hansen's father used to hunt
game once and now whizzes humbly
in his garden, fondling wilted peonies.

His maid is serving us coffee.
The old geezer takes off his leather hat,
saying there are no longer mermaids in the Baltic Sea.

## Musil

Again and again, they come over to see the spiders
Ooh, such pretty things, why don't you hold them in your hand?
Or
I never expected a vermin-hating man
Would keep something so disgusting

Because
I have no influence over it
They must also be intrigued by Musil's dusty *Man Without Qualities*
Anywhere I turn – spider webs, hairy arms
I don't know what they want from me.

## Silent Night, Holy Night

I'm all alone on the planet
and then suddenly: Fuck me,
Johnny, fuck me, or I'll
flake out here! I put on THE TRIFFIDS:
MY BABY THINKS SHE'S A TRAIN

## To Two Beautiful Mulatto Girls Watching The Painting "Five Stories Of Success And Self-Determination"

Looking at you, I think
of blind snakes
and Lorca's
oranges.

All this snow
has made me
mad.

## A Hovercraft

On that hard day, me and Allan
on a canal in Copenhagen.
The green bench, same as ever...
Will something happen at last?
Finally a man jogs by and we
laugh for he barely lifts his feet,
gliding just like a hovercraft!

## Avocado Butter

Look at the horizon.
The sea is ascending into grey clouds.
It's over. Soon the creature exchange will begin.

Meanwhile, the hour of love has struck. Birds,
chinchillas,
a plastered dolphin making a pass at the salesman's sister…

Andropause is not our concern. (Picasso fathered a child at

eighty.)

## The Commandery (At The Brothel At Christine's)

I've got used to it. No, I never have got used to it.
It drives me mad. (That's why I took to drink again.)
I've had this buzzing in my ears lately.

Do you know Botswana is trying to get rid of its elephants?
And what do I think?
So much hassle
what with the tax and the low-protein diet.

Poor Jacques de Molay. They still do
remember him. No one remembers my father.
No one remembers Ares either. What an unjust
disproportion! (They were never very good at mind games.)

But
it has all been planned beforehand anyway. We've been tricked.
You pay for love everywhere. That's why I took to drink again.

**Far Away (*Oedipus Rex*)**

Stravinsky... Then someone asks about writers from Calcutta.
And then *Oedipus Rex* again. Before the new phases
of the moon begin and I snatch you again with my gnarled
hands.

**\*\*\***

The nine holes of my mortal friend.
Some of them decent, but at least two
You'd do better not to mention aloud.
There are queasy individuals among us,
You wouldn't want them to throw up.
Every hole has a special job to take care of.
They are all connected, with me too.
For these are the nine holes of my mortal body.
And one more thing, most vital of all:
Who sees them clearly, loses social respect.
And another thing, most vital too:
Who sees them clearly, fears his own shadow.
And one last thing to wind up:
Who sees them clearly, no longer *is*.

**Caution, The Robots Are Come!**

I discovered the first when he handed me the change.
(Bloody baldhead,
he didn't give a damn about the banknotes!)

Number two had a drink with me on the staircase.
He didn't speak any human language.
He just purred like a well-fed cat.

**A kind of dilemma (resulting
in an unjust distribution of food which in turn causes a
general
hyperactivity of shadows
and
that's how OFFensive literature begins)**

In a publisher's note I read that my poems
were *poetry on the sheer prose of life* –
*on insects,*
*tangerines,*
*birds,*
*emaciated men suffering from cancer,*
*a beggar,*
*visiting one's mother,*
*everyday activities.*

As it happens, I am also the author of the following lyrical work:

*Let us start again from scratch:*
*I'm the target of their archery practice*
*and all I do is… smile*
*nicely! I yank the arrow out*
*of my ass and wait politely*
*for a new one. Is this*
*what you really want???*

The question now is, how should we classify this one?
Together with the ones on
insects
tangerines,
birds,
emaciated men suffering from cancer,
a beggar,
visiting one's mother,
everyday activities?

Oh, the allure of symbiosis! It would be, then, a poem on an insect
gorging on tangerines

who is the target practice of emaciated men suffering from cancer,
while a wise raven is devising revenge.

And all this
as seen by a beggar, a narcissist loser who,
after another visit to his mother, was sent to a
psychoneurodefinitelydonotgointhere ward
but was by accident assigned to a barrack full of patients with a
very different
diagnosis
& preferences…
It could also be a poem about an arrow yanked from the ass
in the evening, after sunset.

If that were the case, the note should be expanded:
*poetry on the sheer prose of life —*
*on insects,*
*tangerines,*
*birds,*
*emaciated men suffering from cancer,*
*a beggar,*
*visiting one's mother,*
*everyday activities,*
*an arrow yanked from the ass*

(in the evening, after sunset).

## Kings Of The Night

Not thugs, more like
ancient bats crouching in fear.

Pulling out flasks on the sly,

They have women drive pink umbrellas
into their crotches.

**Unofficial Code Of Conduct**

Renoir once again, though there have been
poems about him and because of this ladies
shed copious tears and an art connoisseur
ran around in bewilderment with a stomach-ache, etc.

The poor wretch Renoir again, then:
granted, his old age wasn't all too
rosy, he had a hard time like every other
ailing OAP, but why

does it always come to a breach of conduct
when you mention, God forbid, that his father
was a tailor and had the eyes of a common sadist?
(*Portrait of Renoir's Father*, 1869; Saint Louis, City Art Museum.)

### Colonic Cancer Patients

Emaciated men suffering from colonic cancer
watch wasps in silence.

Today one is nimble and fat.

## She Said: You Resemble An Ape

Later I saw you bang your head against the sour
air of the cage.
It may seem ridiculous –

Despite the oil-resistant
antielectrostatic boots
that you had boasted of since you finally gave up
the snake-skin boots,

Just because you resemble an ape

You decided to burn *Winnie the Pooh*.

## Spring

plan A
    to hang myself
plan B
    to hang myself
plan C
    to weather the winter
        and in spring
            to hang myself

## Urbino

*Palazzo Ducale, Raphael's house…* The epicenter
of the Renaissance.

You break your story halfway through.

*And here, granite, and no ornaments.*
Panting.

Staring transfixed at your thighs is a North European

mammal.

## Rhododendrons

Rhododendrons absorb
the fumes of the roasting pig:

Do I remember the Vietnam war?
No, I don't.

Would I like some meat?
No, thanks. No meat for me.

What I am doing here, then?
Watering the rhododendrons.

## A Sudden Realisation

This bearded guy in the Turkish bistro
who's showing me the door has spent
30 years in the back kitchen, shoving
lamb from plate to bloody plate.

## Dodo

The islanders lick snow with respect.
No occultist in sight. (The feuding cats
are out of the game.) The dodo could not
adjust

(hot ocean steamed off the stone floor at our place).
I can no longer walk.
Here's my skipping rope!
I roll about in a jar,

next to a flawed cherry
and an autistic beetle.

\*\*\*

was it worth it, getting fags at a kiosk
and smoking the whole lot at a crazy
pace, washing them down with the cheapest
wine there is and then dying of a heart attack?
— I asked the guy in the freezer next to mine

and was it worth it, lying down in bed,
smoochy smoochy, night darlin', perfect
digestion and, with soft Indian music
in your ears, passing away in sleep? — he answered
my question with a question.

## A Rash Decision

A friend of mine suddenly switched to sweet
herring. And mastered the word HVEDEBRØDSDAG!

He announced he was now a true Dane
(got himself a summer job as a waiter at Tivoli)

and would only speak Danish from now on,
no exceptions… HVORDAN HAR DU DET?

Even to his mother-in-law, a 100-kilo
tough lady from the town of Lublin!

I told him he really needed
to reconsider.

## In A Christianshavn Pub, Larsen Talks About His Undeservedly Settled Life

I know what you mean, Larsen. Just like me,
you are now a big fat pig stuffing yourself
with salted peanuts and reading gossip columns
about the Austrian Nazis who dominate
the Internet with impunity.
Don't worry, Larsen! This could happen
to anybody! Fucking hell… Just look at the sad-faced
boys in orange jumpsuits, trimming shrubs
on the moat since morning. Would you like to have
anything to do with them again?

## Suggestion For A June Activity

In how many languages do birds communicate?
Are we the only civilization in the universe?
Why are so many fools born each summer?

Let us put these questions together in a sort of
Good luck chain letter and send them to our loved ones.
Surprising answers will start arriving in a week.

## Lars's Sudden Confession

If for the last twelve months I hadn't paid
regular visits to that whore on Istedgade,
I could afford a painting by Wilfredo Lam
at an auction today. As it is, I've become
a connoisseur of a totally run-down
old ho!

## Dreaming Of Dragons
## (Mixed Media On Canvas)

1.
Francis would add more water.
2.
Treacherous pewter, Germanic symbols… The climate changes slowly bring about hallucinations.
3.
The second-hand stuff seller noticed a juggler in the left-hand corner.
*The juggler then challenged Arnaut Daniel.*
(Feeling silly now? That's not how you work your way up to gold teeth and a villa in Tuscany.)
4.
Nature painters hang themselves too.
5.
What we need is resistance poetry.
Guts!
6.
Are known to be local parts of the priest and the rhinoceros.
7.
I had no idea (the male lover dressed up as an intellectual).
Leaving grayness, you enter an even greater lack of contrast.
You'll walk through a wall, remaining underground.
8.
A prisoner will be despised.
9.
And you'll open one eye in the baths innkeeper's room.
10.
Love manoeuvres?
11.
In the baths' owner's room.

## No. 2

The first one I fell in love with
wouldn't stop talking about
her passion for cooking chicken's stomachs.

Nothing helped there, not even
listening to Brahms late at night.
The love was quick to vanish.

The second ate tulips before going to bed.
That's when I started to think back
on the first one.

## Mr. Cullen's Raid

Mr. Cullen from Texas, USA, murdered a tree.
He poured four litres of strong poison on an Austin oak tree
Under which the whites shook hands with the natives in 1836.
Paul Cullen will spend 9 long years in jail, but he accomplished
His task superbly: he killed the last, inconvenient witness!

## A Northern Trail

1.
Love is but a delusion. Nature keeps making us realize it.
The skeleton of a smallish mammal. Why did it have to
Be you? (It must have been a pretty specimen once.) I know
You don't like stuffed animals. Vulpes? The trees are thinning.

2.
Yet love it is? You have to nourish it to survive.
You're not going to leave me here all alone, are you?
Have you heard foxes have vertical pupils? Eyes are an abyss
Of greatness and pettiness. (Always so self-assured...)

3.
I'm not talking about survival, but loneliness.
He was the weaker specimen so he was eliminated.
Is this still love, though? Would you also make love to me
If things were otherwise? Oh, come on, get a grip.

4.
Your holistic view on the whole is unsuitable here.
And do cover this ugly skeleton with earth.

## SKY-BLUE HEADS

10 litres of half-price acrylic ocean!
We'll give it the caption SKY-BLUE HEADS
and do a tour of the Jutland countryside.
Just think, the grim breeders of pigs
and ostriches…

We'll tell them our paintings help
to harvest wheat but they're really best for
mating under (we'll add fertility planners
along with mysterious charts
involving the full moon.)

Then we'll pack up and head off to some exotic island!
To search for a new version of pantheism.

## Revisiting A Lover From Five Months Ago

Instead of You – something very much
like You.
(No screaming.)

A phone call later:
How was it this time?

Pick new lovers with good care.
Sex with hallucinations is worse
than nicotine.

A plump blonde will be
quickest of all to deal with.
If you are
of middle height.

That's what the astro-scholars say.

Brunettes are dangerous,
they can stick in your head
for 200 long days.

You can drink filtered water, but still
you're in for a nightmare
and humiliation.

## Dharma

Close your eyes, you'll see a vast field
of tulips in bloom.

Now open.

You'll see sparrows taking peeks
at ripe sunflowers.

## A Strange Je Ne Sais Quoi

Those who once climbed the tallest pines
Can't seem to please the earth again.
Look, here come the clowns,
Say the shopkeepers, now fatter than ever,
When they pass by.

Must be a strange je ne sais quoi that controls it.

One man loses all time and again, while another buys
A mirror,
And later an old clock,
And then a young girl sits in his lap
And in drives a truck loaded with bricks for a new hen coop.

## Toll-gate

You fools,
do you think you have nothing in common

with the horsefly and the tomato seller
whose daughters prematurely lost their teeth?

Do you delude yourselves you're made of marble
like antique sculptures?

## How You Pulled Mary S.

(No 5, A major, K. 219)
Lima's in ruins again.

## Mice

We only know them from descriptions in books.
They have to be small, fluffy and quite cunning, right? Or is that
the Midsummer?
Can't go without an old cat. (All the people who could be trusted
were annihilated).

Experienced enough so as not to be scared by fireworks in Iraq?

You propose lovemaking al fresco. Never mind even
bloodthirsty leeches.
Because we're unstuck from our own skin.
We think that the sun was installed yesterday by Mcorso,
The boring mis-en-scène guy from first floor.

## A Rarity

I was a svelte car
with a long name and many digits
funny but this short episode in my life
fascinated a host of doctors so much
that they wanted to hear nothing of my other incarnations
only asked again and again how much I consumed per 100.

## Mao

Mao Tse-Tung ordered the extermination
of the sparrows. He had several covetous
mistresses and a huge belly
which enabled him to float
effortlessly above bewildered,
skinny divers!

## Phosphorite Mining

Don't lick my skin,
look me
in the face.

**(Poem)**

The desiccated man over there, gatherer of seeds, in the pen with
his turkeys,
has never
learnt to use the spoon or been with a woman.
No one seems to mind that, no one

but the old medic. No, wrong there,
the medic is OK with it too. The All-Seeing Eye, then?
Someone must be his sworn enemy,
mustn't they?

## Heartfelt Advice From A Nuuk Fortuneteller

First give your
Money away
To bums.

Then do
A headstand
And wait:

A sparrow
Will show up
Or a policeman.

## Expeditor

*In memory of F.W.J. Schelling*

Derry has just lost to Dublin.
Will the sea level rise now?
Thousands of men lost their teeth and wives today.
Benny S., for one.
(*Coinciding powers, swarming drives…*)

Meanwhile, my horse – the number 5,
my horse, Expeditor, do they know,
I wonder, that ejaculation inevitably leads
to disaster? But we act in the light
of the law of the Amager island:

Expeditor will surely complete the run, leaving
Clark and the farting Black Goodman behind…
Benny, I'll treat you to gold fronts soon,
Though in my current, empirical life
I cannot upgrade from potency to the act itself.

## 96 Syndrome

The day like a single glove on a fence
(Mrs. A. was run over by a train).

Poor English cows…
They ruined our civilization,
they did.

But we'll all meet in heaven
anyway.

## Therapy

Larsen's out on the playground,
Flying kites with
The kids…

Remember how yesterday
He ran around
With a flick-knife?

Today he's back to normal,
Only looking like a halved
Pumpkin.

**Our Flying Objects**

Early on we watch dragonflies and butterflies
We're still young and enchanted by
flies feasting in a sugar bowl

Next, we shoot our slings at sparrows
Then keep canaries as pets and so
learn to love animals

First sex rightly brings nightingales
to mind, and maturity – a regular
feeding of pigeons

In the end only owls seem intriguing
We sit sulkily at the window and all
that lives pisses us off

## The Demons Of Márquez

Sierva María haunts him in his dreams.
*Vade retro! Vade retro!* (The hens mate with the parrots…)
Her long white hair grows over her old
woman's eyebrows.

The main thing is to wake up again.
And go back
to the uncanopied bed.

## Concord

Warm earth. Our mouths are kissed
by mosquitoes that need their drink.
(Apparently we're one big happy family!)

The waters of the canal on Christianshavn
gently rock snoring stars. We're so close
to heaven today...

## A Long Friendship

Sorry, but I prefer some things unsaid.
If I did tell you all that
Our long friendship would instantly

Turn into a quick and transient love.
You'd be sorry then and rightly put the blame
On me.

## The Breathing Organs Of Fish

Let's get a move on

before they start
looking suggestive.

**According To The Enclosed Brochure**

Three pills were said to help, or at least do no harm.
Still, after I took two, unpleasant things started to happen.
Suddenly Homer disappeared from my memory and then
thieves walked out through curtained windows
with a week's supply of food.
Loss. Anger. Misunderstanding.
The chemistry promised relief
but instead
I landed myself in new trouble.

I am now thinking of changing my prescription.
The thought of upping the dose excites me.
I have always been much too impatient.
(I could have kept the pet macaw but I was obsessed with
betrayal…)
I took the third pill.
And then the fourth.
I half-close my eyes.
Someone's hand creeps up to the tin of jasmine tea.
I wait.

## Anarchy and Tuna

a group of anarchists throwing a Molotov cocktail bought
for social services money
calculate the cost of finishing off
one policeman
you have to budget cleverly, as there has to be enough left
for canned tuna and lemon
canned tuna is just the thing for a rebel: a cheap foodstuff
that makes you go forever!
state officials regularly pay the anarchists
their dole and in so doing support anarchy
officials and anarchists supposedly being
two fiercely antagonistic worlds!
you can't mention an anarchist in front of an official unless you
want him to have a fit of nervous hiccups,
or a white shirt tucked into grey pants
in front of an anarchist, unless you want him to get his knife
it's hard to be an official,
it's equally hard to be an anarchist,
but it's shit manners to be an anarchist
in a welfare state

## Renoir and Van Gogh

Renoir was not naïve: *Painting is there*
*To decorate walls.*
Conversation... The Isshidan Garden in Kyoto.
Tapies's canvases in stone? Or a poster,
maybe? *El Quixote* de Antonio Saura.
Since Saura died – there's only Tapies!
Too many reproductions here, then, and gap-toothed
prostitutes from Thailand.
Barcelona? It's so far away.
In Copenhagen, only a billiards table,
Jacobsen's forks and chairs.
No use denying it, I do love cheap jewelry
and expensive, pre-war silver,
and I've always felt at my optimum in the city.
That's why I'd like to pop out to the country.
Because –
I'd like to see a horse again,
though, to be honest, I've no idea why...
Horses can be quite dangerous, after all.
Oh, we also have Kierkegaard!
You mustn't forget.
Camus was under the influence, no doubt.
A horse instead of a smoke, a must at my age,
Nothing more for me now but subtle sunflowers.
And here goes Renoir again: *For me, a painting has to be*
*something nice,*
*something joyful,*
*something pretty.* I disagree.
Let's take the jittery Van Gogh,
for example:
*I pay for my art*
*with the risk of life,*
*it took half my mind away.*
Failures. Women in flowing dresses
and old shawls.
Van Gogh. Renoir.
They were right.

(We'll be carted
To the morgue soon.) *Adios, amigo borracho!*
Their portraits are immortal, as long as
I look at them.

\* \* \*

You wonder why you find yourself facing everyday ascetic
practice and reading the old stuff by Stephen King?

Because we were out of luck again and the keys
were not right for that car, property of your wife, who is down

with bronchitis (I never even knew you were married),
neither for the other, which some clueless plainclothes dogs

parked right next to hers.

## Homage to Short Stays

Maybe it's because of riots in Albania
or how the clay god Ganesha
affects us. I should count
on nothing pleasant today.

(I'm even miffed at the sweet mangoes
you bought at the Pakistani's yesterday.)
Looks like these are the only reasons
I called my last drawing *Loneliness*.

"The disease of civilization...", sighs
the gallery owner, upset.
I might as well have
called it *Eyes*.

It would amount to the same thing.

## Love, Ecology and Moon

We listen to the faraway singing
of fighter-planes: the Moon sect has not
found our suburban hideout yet!

A momentary idyll… Here, all that matters
are white shells and birds emerging
from pure clouds.

You mean so much to me, more than
the nuclear plant at Barsebäck.

## Henrietta on a Date

A grasshopper hid behind the basket belonging
to Henrietta. Stripped naked, she tears down the hot leaves
and fools around with a corn cob.

Sweaty all over, she waits for her man, who
is not coming for another 4 months, not until
he has completed his clerical training in Odense.

### The Castle

Cats' eyes and honeymooning
Russians. On the wall, the immortal
MICKY FROM SWINDON!

The last concierge was be-
headed in 1600…

**(Let's go back to the mainland**

before they lock us in a living room
full of stuffed lizards
&
1/32-scale airship models)

# ABOUT THE AUTHOR

**Grzegorz Wróblewski**, born in 1962 in Gdansk and raised in Warsaw, has been living in Copenhagen since 1985. He has published ten volumes of poetry and three collections of short prose pieces in Poland; three books of poetry, a book of poetic prose and an experimental novel (translations) in Denmark; and a book of selected poems in Bosnia-Herzegovina, as well as a selection of plays. His work has been translated into fifteen languages.

The English translations of his poems and/or plays have appeared in *London Magazine, Poetry London, Magma Poetry, Parameter Magazine, Poetry Wales, The Delinquent, Chicago Review, 3rd bed, Eclectica, Mississippi Review, Absinthe: New European Writing, Common Knowledge, Word Riot, Practice: New Writing + Art, The Mercurian – A Theatrical Translation Review, Lyric, CounterPunch, Exquisite Corpse, Guernica, Jacket Magazine, Otoliths, Cambridge Literary Review, 3:AM Magazine, Past Simple, Denver Quarterly, Colorado Review, AGNI Online, Words Without Borders, Shampoo, Seneca Review, Postmodern Culture, West Wind Review* and in the following anthologies: *Altered State: The New Polish Poetry* (Arc Publications, Todmorden, UK 2003), *Carnivorous Boy Carnivorous Bird* (Zephyr Press, Brookline, USA 2004), *A Generation Defining Itself – In Our Own Words* (MW Enterprises, USA 2007).

Selected poems *Our Flying Objects* (Equipage Press, Cambridge, UK 2007), new and selected poems *A Marzipan Factory* (Otoliths, Rockhampton, Australia 2010), and prose poems *Kopenhaga* (Zephyr Press, USA 2013).

His chapbooks to date are: *These Extraordinary People* (erbacce-press, Liverpool, UK 2008) and *Mercury Project* (Toad Press, Claremont, USA 2008), *A Rarity* (Červená Barva Press, W. Somerville, USA, 2009).

## ABOUT THE TRANSLATOR

**Agnieszka Pokojska** is a freelance translator and editor, tutor in literary translation at the Jagiellonian University in Krakow, and author of a number of articles on translation. Her translations into Polish include poems by Seamus Heaney, Robert Pinsky and Derek Walcott. Her translations of Grzegorz Wróblewski's poetry appeared in the anthology *Carnivorous Boy Carnivorous Bird*, in *Lyric Poetry Review*, *West Wind Review*, *Eclectica*, *Jacket Magazine*, *The Journal*, *Cambridge Literary Review*, *Past Simple*, *Words Without Borders*, *The Delinquent*, *3:AM Magazine*, *Postmodern Culture*, *Exquisite Corpse*, *Otoliths* and *Poetry Wales* and most recently in the chapbook *A Rarity* published by Červená Barva Press.